LADIES

NO MORE

FISHING

Ladies No More Fishing

Ladies No More Fishing

Copyright © 2000

Shiela Y. Harris

First Printing 2012

Unless otherwise indicated all scripture notations are taken from the Holy Bible, New International Version ® Copyright © 1973, 1978, 1984 by International Bible Society. Used by permission of Zondervan Publishing House, All rights reserved.

The "NIV" and "New International Version" trademarks are registered in the United States Patent and Trademark Office by the International Bible Society. Use of either trademark requires permission of International Bible Society.

Scripture quotations marked KJV are taken from the King James Version of the Bible.

All rights reserved. No part of this publication may be reproduced, stored in a retrieval system or transmitted in any form or by any means, electronic, mechanical, photocopying, recording or otherwise, without written consent from the author or publisher.

ISBN: 9780967931210

Shiela Y. Harris

DEDICATION

This book is dedicated to women of God everywhere. Be encouraged and patient as you wait on God for your mate. Don't exude anxiousness going before God rushing into a relationship, He knows what is best for us.

Ladies No More Fishing

Shiela Y. Harris

INTRODUCTION

While working in ministry teaching and fellowshipping with women, it became apparent that we are ever more desperate for marriage. It appears the overall attitude is we want marriage "by any means necessary." The need for male companionship in some cases seems to have a higher priority than our relationship with God. The information in this book is no grand theses but moreover a compilation of common sense rules, personal research, and bible principles for accepting and being a mate.

This is not a word of reproof, but it is a word God has inspired me to share with my readers so we can develop and channel the proper mindset as we prepare ourselves in Christ for matrimony. Neither is this a claim to be an expert on relationships, but by sharing what God has given me through my experiences, successes and failures, personal research, information gathered through years of counseling women and the study of scripture, it will certainly help prevent women from involvement in one-sided relationships because of their misconception and erroneously preconceived ideas for relationship and marriage.

Its purpose is to motivate and encourage the reader to bypass or eliminate all together the hurt and pain, disappointment and heartache that often accompanies, a love gone badly.

As Christians we should not be moved by the things of this world especially with reports that say there is a shortage of men or that one half of the marriages in the United States including the church end in divorce. Our marital destiny lies in the hands of God. What God has for us is for us but it is also our responsibility to be prepared and in position to receive it.

As you read this book I encourage you to do so with a receptive heart and with the attitude that things are about to change for the better.

When we can see things through our spiritual eyes and operate in that realm we prepare ourselves for great things, for victory and success in receiving the things you long for.

Exposure to enormous amounts of negativity regarding relationships in the media, television, movies, newspaper, magazines and, internet are among the many reasons waves of fear consume men and women everywhere. But, as believers in Christ we must stand firm on the prayer of the psalmist David, particularly in Psalms 27:1 (NIV); *"The Lord is my light and my salvation, whom shall I fear. The Lord is the stronghold of my life, of whom shall I be afraid."*

God is with us and wants us to do well, but we must seek God first as in Matthew 6:33; *"But seek first his kingdom and his righteousness, and all these things will be given to you as well."* Once we put *things*, including our desires in perspective allowing God to operate in His divine timing, He will certainly give us the desires of our hearts.

The essence of this book and the important factor for every reader is to know that God's promises are true for every area of our lives. To benefit we must follow God's precepts which are taught in His Word allowing him to hook you up with a godly man as you read and are spiritually enlightened with, "Ladies No More Fishing."

TABLE OF CONTENTS

Chapter	Page No
Chapter 1 Fishers' of Men	9
Chapter 2 What's Your Motive?	21
Chapter 3 Turn On vs. Turn offs	27
Chapter 4 The Self Esteem Factor	31
Chapter 5 The Hygiene Factor	37
Chapter 6 A Match Made In Heaven	39
Chapter 7 Marrying With Children	43
Chapter 8 Ten Principals for Women	45
Chapter 9 Conclusion of the Whole Matter	59

WHY ARE YOU FISHING?

CHAPTER ONE

FISHERS' OF MEN

Men! It has been said we cannot live with or without them. Our agnostic society would have us believe that there is a shortage of men because the ratio is supposedly one man to every five women. A report from the Bureau of Justice Prison Statistics indicates that there are 3,209 Black males; 1,273 Hispanic males and 386 White males per 100,000 males of each ethnic group in the United States prisons. Looking at things in the natural this information would have us believe that there is a shortage of men, especially among minorities.

God's Word states that He will give us the desires' of our heart. We are also instructed to be fruitful and multiply (although many are accomplishing this outside of marriage) this definitely requires a male and female union.

There are scores of Christian women preoccupied with an earnest desire to be married, consequently finding themselves *fishing*, trying to *snag* a mate. According to the scriptures this practice is all wrong. When we find ourselves going to bed at night thinking about finding a man, waking up in the morning with these same thoughts and thinking about this all throughout the day we are preoccupied with finding a mate. What is wrong with this scenario?

The Bible tells us in Proverbs 18:22: *"Whoso findeth a wife findeth a good thing, and obtaineth favor of the Lord."*

What this simply means is the responsibility or initiation of mating in humans relies on the male and women are not to pursue or fish for a mate. To take it even further, when we fish instead of serving as bait we set ourselves up for failure. Women on the prowl, hunting and scavenging for a companion will result in our operating outside the will and purpose of God setting ourselves up for defeat. The term "bait" is not to imply a woman has to be erotically seductive or enticing but it simply suggests a woman need concentrate more on God's promises and plan, knowing He will provide a suitable mate.

Bait references a woman with charm one who is appealing and attractive spiritually and naturally. A noble woman with character as in Proverbs 31:10-31 which describes a woman that fears the Lord and such a woman is also a depiction of wisdom.

Statistically saying there are not enough men according to the ratio of men to women may prove to be true for the unsaved woman but God promised to give us as believers the desires of our heart. Certainly if what we desire, even in the area of marriage, will be used to praise Him, don't you believe He will do it? His Word says so. Matthew 21:22 reads: *"If you believe, you will receive whatever you ask for in prayer."*

God's promises are certainly greater than any statistic. You may be wondering why you haven't been selected. Let's first look at the concept of fishing. When I was a young girl my dad took me fishing on the pier in Redondo Beach, California. We used simple equipment an inexpensive fishing rod and reel. Even in earlier times the best fishing was accomplished using simplistic equipment, a tree branch, string and a hook made from a safety pin or a sharp piece of curved metal. We were not experts by any means but it did help to know what the fish were biting or what bait was being used for the fish we were trying to catch. Different types of bait attracted various species of fish. Some preferred small pieces of jack smelt, others small balls of moist bread and then some even preferred peanut butter and their bait preferences could and would change from day to day. There are also numerous species of fish that can be caught on the pier; perch, rock cod, mackerel, jack smelt, halibut to name a few. The procedure was simple, bait the hook, release the line and sit patiently and quietly and wait for the fish to bite. You could feel the bite on your line; a sudden sharp tugging.

The moment this was felt there was no mistaking it, you knew to jerk hard on your line so you could snag the fish while it is trying to take the bait.

Fishing was never a frustrating event and was rather relaxing even when we did not get a single bite. There was no win or lose, you either caught fish, or you didn't. Whether or not we caught fish we enjoyed the time spent involved on the sport and in most cases, with a little patience we would catch fish.

How often have you said, thought or heard someone else say?

- "I am looking for me a husband."

- "I'm trying to find me a husband"

- "I plan to be married this time next year"

- "I want to have kids before I am 40"

- "I'm going to marry me a preacher"

- "He's got a good job, he's going to be my husband"

- "Girl he's so fine, we could make good looking children"

- "He don't know it but he's going to be my husband"

- "I'm so crazy about that man"

If our desire is to be married and have a family we need to honestly assess our qualities asking and answering these questions: Will I make good bait? What qualities do I have that would make me attractive to a man? Don't answer to quickly because there are scores of woman that think they are all that and two "bags of chips" because of their status in the business world, status in the church, education and physical appearance.

Women will often use these and other standards superficially as a basis of qualification. As females we are usually very specific concerning desired qualifications and characteristics in a man. He must be saved and filled with the Holy Spirit and this is a very good qualification. He must be God fearing, educated and able and willing to work, another good quality. We usually have a long list of requirements for men because we want the perfect mate. But what do you have to offer or give to a relationship? A healthy relationship is much deeper than sexual intimacy. It has more depth than the physical attraction. Do you feel you have been waiting so long that you are willing to bend your prerequisites a *little*? Why would you bend? If you settle for less than what your heart desires, it will be a matter of time that you find yourself unhappy and dissatisfied in the relationship. Sometimes we want a lot more than we have to offer. We want the man to bring everything into the relationship and if he is not all we desire we compare him to what we do desire. We cannot change a person's character and habits and we should not go into a relationship thinking we can.

While on the subject, where in the bible does it instruct women to seek out men who are incarcerated, men who are known to be substance abusers or someone else's husband? Why do we think we have been issued a god license and feel we can change a man whose life is totally contrary to the Word? If you are already married to an unsaved man and you get saved, the bible instructs you on what to do so that he may receive Christ also.

The bible does not support single women to yoke with unbelievers as stated in 2 Corinthians 6:14: *"Do not be yoked together with unbelievers. For what do righteousness and wickedness have in common?*

Or what fellowship can light have with darkness? What harmony is there between? Christ and Belial (Satan)? What does a believer have in common with an unbeliever? What agreement is there between the temple of God and idols?

For we are the temple of the living God. As God has said: "I will live with them and walk among them, and I will be their God, and they will be my people."

Paul was actually warning the Corinthian believers against cooperating with false teachers who were in reality servants of Satan, notwithstanding their charming and persuasive ways. To do so was to become unequally yoked, destroying the harmony and fellowship that united them in Christ. False teachers were accusing Paul of being unjust, destructive and fraudulent, the very things that they were guilty of. There is no room for compromise. Women who are desperate, who walk not in their destiny choose this path and usually regret it in a mighty way. This sort of relationship is not ordained of God, not blessed by God and cannot be successful because God is not the author.

If the biblical process is that a man finds a woman how do we know who is sent of God? Good question! We must be in a true relationship with the Father so that our spiritual discernment enables us to see above our needs. When our needs stand in the way of God's selection we will say "yes" to the first man that comes along. It is essential for our will to be aligned with God's will. If it is not, we will make mistakes that we will live to regret.

We usually have the events of our lives such as marriage, careers and having children predetermined. We want to be married at a certain age and own a home and have our children before a certain time. When the focus is on what we want more than being on what God has for us, or what will please and honor God we often act before God says *yes* and may act adversely when God says *no* or *wait*.

We must realize that *delay* does not always mean *denial*. God knows what is best for us and there can be a number of reasons why He has not sent you a husband. If you want a godly man (and you should), then you must be a godly woman!

What makes you a good catch? What kind of bait are you? Take a few moments and prepare a self-assessment and you do not have to be drop down gorgeous. What qualifications do you possess that causes you to be attractive to the type of man you desire? What are your true qualifications?

Now mind you, I am not speaking necessarily of a man with material possessions, as money, cars, houses or yachts. My reference here is a man with the heart of God. If a man has the heart of God he will love you as much or more than he loves himself. He will provide for you because he loves you and because he wants you to have the things you need and desire. Ephesians 5:22-28, gives explicit instructions for how men are to love their wives and how women are to love their husbands.

Wives, submit to your husbands as to the Lord. For the husband is the head of the wife as Christ is the head of the church, his body, of which he is the Savior. Now as the church submits to Christ, so also wives should submit to their husbands for everything. Husbands, love your wives, just as Christ loved the church and gave himself up for her to make her holy, cleansing her by the washing with water through the word, and to present her to himself as a radiant church, without stain or wrinkle or any other blemish, but holy and blameless. In this same way, husbands ought to love their wives as their own bodies. He who loves his wife loves himself.

The scriptures are not necessarily saying that a woman "obeys" as a child would obey their parent but moreover that there is a mutual submission and a woman submits herself by yielding her rights as the husband and wife submit to one another however, this is not justification for abuse or tyranny. As you continue reading you will see that Paul makes it clear that it is not a one-sided submission but moreover a balanced relationship where they submit one to the other.

Lastly, if a man loves his wife as he loves Christ and himself he more than likely will respect, provide for and cherish her and will not do her harm.

While we are on the subject of provisions it is not a man's responsibility to supply all of our wants but he is responsible to take care of the needs of his family. Should your husband want to shower you with fancy gifts that's good just consider these *things* as icing on the cake. But we should not demand these things of him just because it is our want.

Back to the question (you thought I forgot) what are your characteristics? Are you a virtuous woman? A woman of virtue is moral and righteous and is abstinent while single. She is decent and modest in nature. Sounds wimpy? If this is not your true character, don't be discouraged and do not stop reading this book there is still hope for you. You are not alone and if you are feeling inadequate just keep reading. Most of the information in this book is not new knowledge but prayerfully you will find it enlightening and from this point forward you can be all you need to be in Christ with the material I share with you.

In Proverbs 31: 10-30 we find the description of a *virtuous* woman. As you read this portion of scripture you will find that a virtuous woman is a woman who is highly responsible. She is a nurturer, thrifty, faithful, wise spender, an enterprising person, shows good judgment, raises her children to respect and fear the Lord and does not have an idle mind. She does not waste her time and is not one to watch talk shows all day or gossip on the phone for hours. If your life has not been one of virtue, your true repentance and God's grace can wipe the slate clean.

<u>You can begin anew right now. Say this prayer:</u>
"Lord Jesus, I come before you repenting for the lifestyle I have lived and for all the things I have done that did not line up with your Word. Forgive me and renew in me a spirit of holiness and

sanctification. Give me the patience and restore in me the spirit I need to wait on you for my mate, in Jesus name amen."

There are a large percentage of Christian women that do not feel it is necessary to be celibate and find all kinds of reasons to justify a lifestyle of fornication or adultery (sleeping around).

Actually we sin because we yield to our "fleshly" desires. God's way is celibacy until we are married. The Word does not authorize nor support sin in any form. Let's look at Galatians 5: 16-21:

So I say, live by the Spirit, and you will not gratify the desires of the sinful nature. For the sinful nature desires what is contrary to the Spirit and the Spirit what is contrary to the sinful nature. They are in conflict with each other, so that you do not do what you want. But if you are led by the Spirit, you are not under the law.

The acts of the sinful nature are obvious: sexual immorality, impurity and debauchery; idolatry and witchcraft; selfish ambition, dissensions, factions and envy; drunkenness, orgies, and the like. I warn you, as I did before, that those who live like this will not inherit the kingdom of God.

So you see celibacy is not an option. If we live contrary to the Word of God there are consequences and the greatest consequence is not the reward of heaven but an eternity in hell. The Word says that these acts are obvious and we know what we are doing, we just do not have our flesh under control and find ourselves yielding to the lust of it. Sexual promiscuity has other repercussions, sexually transmitted disease (STD's) such as: AIDS, gonorrhea, syphilis, chlamydia, trichomonas, HPV, genital warts, herpes II, hepatitis C, unplanned pregnancy and more. Some STD's can be fatal to you and your unborn fetus. For one night of sexual frivolity you can end up with a life threatening or terminal illness.

Another mistake women make prior to being hooked is they are *divas* before the wedding and afterwards they slowly develop in to plump, plain and ordinary. While dating we are always neatly groomed and alluringly dressed. With some individuals this may be natural and for others a facade.

Once they become relaxed in matrimony they don't feel it is necessary to continue this practice. While it is true that once we marry we are not out to be caught we should want the fisherman to continue to desire who he has chosen for his wife.

As much as possible you want to continue to be attractive and to display those qualities that made him attracted to you. We all know that with age come gravity and our features change; wrinkles, weight gain, hair loss are all a part of the aging process. But even then you can remain an <u>attractive</u> individual in the eyesight of your mate. This means you do not have to be sloppy and useless or as the bible refers to as a sluggard, a lazy woman.

If your husband is the only one working in the household you should keep your home neat and clean and be crafty enough to prepare meals that are pleasing to the palate. If you have children your time should be spent teaching and caring for them and your home. If you do not know how to cook...learn and if you do not have good parenting skills, take a class. If both spouses are working which is a great percentage in today's households, both parents need to share in the needs of that household and both are certainly to share in the rearing of their children.

Ladies seriously, we do not have to reveal every ounce of flesh on our body to be attractive. Some men will look if you show it, but they will not be interested in bringing you home to meet mom or dad.

Classy women should avoid extremely tight, short, high splits and sheer and skimpy clothing. Not only is it unattractive but it is ungodly. If you attend a Spirit filled church where you might get your dance on or have the floor ministry you need to be covered.

But NO! We want to wear the least amount of clothing and then dance all across the front of the church revealing things that should be privy only to your mirror and you.

Another cute thing we do is purchase clothes for wearing to church and clothes for wearing everywhere else. If it is not appropriate to wear to church you should probably leave it in the store.

Just as it is important for us not to dress too provocatively neither should we walk around looking like a matronly nun. Our clothes should be clean and hair should be neatly groomed and the use of a little make-up is advisable. Being saved does not mean we should look homely and unattractive. Dress tastefully and use a little make-up and some sweet smelling fragrances like, Victoria Secret and Bath & Body are great places to start. Remember Proverbs 31:30; *Charm is deceptive, and beauty is fleeting; but a woman who fears the Lord is to be praised.* Boringly plain is not necessarily the approach to beautiful and or attractiveness.

Additionally, we should remember when we ask God for something he does not need our help to manifest it. Stop being impatient and wait on the Lord. Oftentimes we ask God for things that we are not quite ready for and consequently he has to prepare us first before he can bestow us with His blessings, and then we must be in position to receive them. As for the gift of a husband we need to be physically, spiritually and emotionally ready for a partner in marriage. We can't carry "baggage" into a relationship. Old baggage will destroy it before you can get started. We should not enter into a relationship with wounds and hurts from relationships past. We must enter into it with a clean emotional slate. Start fresh. By all means get delivered.

Let's go back a bit and deal with <u>you</u>. Why do you want to be married? Is it because all of your friends are getting married, or because you want to have a family by a certain age? Is it a goal you set for yourself, or is it so you can have the wedding of a lifetime?

Is it because you want a license for sex so you will not have to worry about celibacy? Why do you want to be married? Your expectations certainly determine your mindset when you enter into matrimony. You should first LOVE each other.

Not a love based on physical attraction or euphoria but a godly love. Love unconditional is crucial because it allows <u>two</u> the opportunity to become <u>one</u> and grow together in Christ.

God's promises are true but they are conditional. We must live and abide in His will in order to receive His blessings. The longer women have to wait the more desperate they seem to become. If we are not careful our attitude about waiting can cause us to lose sight of God. We will then concentrate more on what we are waiting for rather than whom we are waiting on. God knows the desires of our heart and He also knows what we need and when we need it. The more desperate we are the longer the wait and the more agitated we become until we are consumed with our wants.

Once we understand biblical principles in regards to relationships and marriage, we can patiently wait on God and prepare ourselves by staying in position for him to send our soul mate. There has to be a definite change in our way of thinking and we must be receptive to doing things God's way.

So I say to ladies everywhere, we don't have to go on the prowl nor do we have to be mistresses of seduction. All we need do is make our petition known to God, believe in the promises of God, live by his Word and patiently wait for him to answer. Let God do it!

ASK YOURSELF, WHAT'S MY MOTIVE?

CHAPTER TWO

WHAT'S YOUR MOTIVE?

We need to further discuss what we have to offer a relationship in comparison to what it is we want out of it. What attributes do we have that qualifies us as a good mate? Usually, when thinking about a question like this we either put ourselves on a pedestal or we may feel just the opposite, that we do not deserve anything good and descent. But seriously think about the attributes that would define you as a virtuous woman as discussed in Proverbs 31.

You have an education, that's good; you have your hair, eyebrows and nails groomed bi-monthly, that's good too. You are active in ministry and regularly attend church including Bible Study, saved and Holy Ghost filled. But what qualifies you to be a person that is ready for marriage?

Most times, we view marriage as glamorous and as a status symbol. There is the extravagant wedding, you feel your life is complete because you have a home with a husband and maybe there will be children. Do you want a husband because of status or want a provider, a partner you can legally be intimate with? Have you met someone that you truly love and can continue loving (for rich or for poor, in sickness and in health) until death comes between you? Again I emphasize marriage is so much deeper.

Let's review some things we need to bring into a relationship. It **must first** be realized that we cannot *find* the right man; it is not our job to find a man. This is not the way God planned it so if we go fishing, we may catch something but it may be a barracuda in disguise. Remember I stated in the first chapter that there are a lot of different species of fish. The barracuda is one of the fiercest of fish. It is an ugly savage fish with a narrow muscular body, a long cruel mouth and yellowish green eyes. When it feeds it circles a school of fish until they huddle together in fear and then dives in the midst, biting and slashing with saw like teeth.

They will strike at most moving objects; even people have been known to be attacked by them. This is what a lot of women end up with when they go fishing for mates. Some catch an ugly, mean barracuda man.

We are looking at desirable qualities and attributes so let's continue. We even tell God in our prayer petition what kind of man we want. We want someone kind and tender, gentle, compassionate, loving, caring, sincere and peaceful. Then the list goes on as we desire a man that is intelligent and well educated with a good job -- a man who is generous, affectionate, humorous, trustworthy and of course, strong, handsome and a passionate, romantic lover. We know how to tell God to do His job. Yes we do! If God does not move in our time then we cast our line (oftentimes making a fool of ourselves) and begin to fish.

We cast our lines and fish in every lake and stream, in oceans and ponds, rivers and brooks. We cast our bait (flesh and seduction) and we fish and fish and fish until we hook a man and then say, "God gave me this man," or tell the poor victim that, "God showed me you would be my husband." This is serious denial and you are lying on God.

Is it fair for God to give us something that we are not? Is it fair for him to give us a responsibility we are not ready for? Are you loving and kind, (what about PMS)? Are you generous, what happens when money gets tight and you may need to forfeit a few luxuries? Are you easy to forgive or do you carry a grudge and go on *lock down* when there is a disagreement? Can you be sensitive and unselfish? A delay may be God trying to work on our character and spirit so we can become all that we are looking for in a man. When we exclude God from the selecting process our fishing will only hook disappointment and disaster.

Women of God often miss out on who God has for us because we lack patience. We take the first man that comes along and end up in such a mess, even to the point where the relationship of our choosing can be emotionally and physically abusive. How do we end up taking care of men with no employment history, no skills or intentions of working, living in your house and driving your car (just thought I would ask)?

This may seem harsh but it is important that we realize that anything that is not of God is of Satan so when a relationship is not of God it is of Satan, there is no in between. When we hook up with an adversary of the devil we have snagged ourselves something...Freddy Krueger or Jason's first cousin. You star in your own personal movie, "A Nightmare on Your Street."

We use such absurd reasons for matrimony desperation; such as, our biological clock is ticking and we need to be married because we are not getting any younger. Remember delay usually means there is some preparation that needs to be made on our part so we can measure up to our own desires.

Our motive should be that of wanting to be united with someone that God has chosen for us. Our spiritual Father is omnipotent (all-powerful), omniscient (all-knowing) and omnipresent (every-where at the same time). We should always want our steps ordered by God. As believers in Christ we are responsible for living according to the Word of God in every area of our lives. *"Trust in the Lord with all thine heart; and lean not unto thine own understanding. In all thy ways acknowledge him and he shall direct thy path," Proverbs 3:5-6.* Matthew Henry's commentary explains this text as such:

We must therefore trust in the Lord with all our hearts and we must believe that he is able to do what he will, wise to do what is best, and good, according to his promise, to do what is best for us, if we love him, and serve him. We must, with an entire submission and satisfaction, depend upon him to perform all things for us, and not lean to our own understanding, as if we could, by any forecast of our own, without God, help ourselves, and bring our affairs to a good issue. In all our conduct we must be diffident of our own judgment, and confident of God's wisdom, power, and goodness, and therefore must follow Providence and not force it.

We must not only in our judgment believe that there is an over-ruling hand of God ordering and disposing of us and all our affairs, but we must solemnly own it, and address ourselves to him accordingly. We must ask his leave, and not design anything but what we are sure is lawful. We must ask his advice and request direction from him, not only when the case is difficult (when we know not what to do, no thanks to us that we have our eyes up to him), but in every case, be it ever so plain. We must ask success of him, as those who know the race is not to the swift. We must refer ourselves to him as one from whom our judgment proceeds, and patiently, and with a holy indifference, wait his award. In all our ways that prove direct, and fair, and pleasant, in which we gain our point to our satisfaction, we must acknowledge God with thankfullness. In all our ways that prove cross and uncomfortable, and that are hedged up with thorns, we must acknowledge God with submission. For our encouragement to do this, it is promised, "He shall direct thy paths, so that thy way shall be safe and good and the issue happy at last." Those that put themselves under a divine guidance shall always have the benefit of it. God will give them that wisdom which is profitable to direct, so that they shall not turn aside into the by-paths of sin, and then will himself so wisely order the event that it shall be to their mind, or (which is equivalent) for their good.

By now it should be clear and is scripturally proven that the selection process is not up to us. Whether we accept whom God sends and are able to discern what is of God is up to us. Remember that Proverbs 18:22 states, *"He who finds a wife a wife finds what is good and receives favor from the Lord."* So our motive or desire for marriage should not be for selfish or foolish gain.

In order for us to know who is sent from God we must have an intimate relationship with the Father. We must have an active prayer and study life. The Holy Spirit reveals God's wisdom to us and God's Spirit helps us to understand and accept God's Word as the truth. So in order to discern the things of God we must be filled with the Holy Spirit. As believers we have the benefit of having the Holy Spirit teach us as we read and study God's Word.

We can know what God has for us by reading and applying His Word and then by obeying and applying His truths to our lives, which helps us to recognize the deceit of the prince of darkness. How often do we read the bible and apply its truths? This is of utter importance to the believer, to the one seeking God for a mate.

As we end this chapter take a few moments and think about your motive. From the information you have read thus far do you sense there are some personal characteristics that need change? Should you reassess your motives and your relationship with the Father? Now would be a good time to take an honest assessment so as you continue reading there will not be any known flaws to hinder you receiving your mate.

DO YOU HAVE WHAT IT TAKES TO...?

CHAPTER THREE

TURN ON VS. TURN OFFS

Some ministries have taught the use of makeup, pressed or relaxed hair, garments worn down to the ankle defines a woman's level of holiness. Unfortunately this veneer did not prevent unwed mothers nor did it help change the unfriendly and judgmental attitudes among its women. This is not meant to make mockery of anyone's religious practices but this kind of foolishness does not make one holy nor does it sanctify us before God. There are no great deeds nor can sanctimonious modes of dressing sanctify or save us.

Ephesians 2:5-4: But because of his great love for us, God who is rich in mercy, made us alive with Christ even when we were dead in transgressions – is by grace you have been saved.

Ephesians 2:8: For it is by grace you have been saved – through faith and this is not from yourselves it is the gift of God – not by works so that no one can boast.

Though modesty is essential Holiness is a lifestyle and not a mode of dress. It is our heart-felt belief in the death and resurrection of Christ that saves us. I repeat…holiness is a lifestyle and not a mode of dress.

In the same manner, because we are saved our mode of dress should be in good taste and modest, and not necessarily homely and plain, there is a difference. There is no sin in wanting to look attractive. Men are attracted to, sweet fragrances, good personal hygiene, light make-up, feminine character, nicely styled hair, trendy styles that compliment any self-assured intelligent women.

These are a natural turn on. Unfortunately there are women in church who are a natural turn-off. Sloppy dressing, hair uncombed, poor personal hygiene, boisterous, wearers of intrusively heavy make-up, insecure gossiping women, low and no class women, ghetto fabulous women which all falls under the heading of very unattractive women.

We must be saved, holy-ghost filled women of noble character, virtuous, wise and crafty women that walk by faith. These are the things that insure us being viewed as a woman that God can entrust into a relationship with a godly man.

<u>Proverbs 31:25-27</u> Strength and honor are her clothing; and she shall rejoice in time to come. She openeth her mouth with wisdom; and in her tongue is the law of kindness. She looketh well to the ways of her household, and eateth not the bread of idleness.

The Word is saying that the opposite of strength and dignity is to be clothed with shame and disgrace. A woman of virtue is free from worry and anxiety. She is one who realizes that honor comes through humility and fearing the Lord.

An equally important point is beauty is not necessarily all wrapped up in the physical package. Some women have a natural beauty that make up only enhances while others have to work at being or appearing beautiful. But there is an old saying, "beauty's only skin deep." This is true with supernatural beauty which comes from the heart. It is possible for one to be physically gorgeous and yet appear unattractive because their ways and mannerisms are ugly. Our standards regarding the *"ideal woman"* change from generation to generation even our ideas about beauty. When one's beauty is from the heart regardless of their physical appearance she is indeed a beautiful woman, one who God will bless, honor and favor.

We certainly can learn a lot from women in the bible. Women like Rebekah and Sarah. Rebekah was selected for Isaac by God through the prayers of a servant. Sarah was faithful to God and was submitted to her husband and him to her for over 100 years. She knew that nothing was impossible for God. Her waiting on God to give her a son is a prime example that God works not according to our schedule and our help is not needed in the process. God is true to His Word and does not lie and all of His promises are yes. Even when we make bad choices God does not interfere but instead, we may have to live with the consequences of these choices and if he steps in it is not necessarily to rescue us but to carry out his plan for us.

Two other familiar biblical women are Mary, the mother of Jesus and Elizabeth, mother of John. Mary had no intimacy before marriage and until the birth of Jesus. She continued to be a faithful wife to Joseph and even remained a celibate widow after his death.

Elizabeth and Zacharias were old and childless but because Zacharias loved his wife, he did not divorce her even though her childlessness was grounds for such. Despite their age she never stopped praying and believing for a child. This was very important to Jewish women. Elizabeth and Zachariah were righteous and patient believers and though they had years of disappointment her faith did not weaken. Although Zacharias doubted and his mouth was shut for six-months because of his unbelief, they were able to maintain a close relationship with God and with each other through many years of waiting.

Patience is important. What happens during our waiting period? Desperation sets in because of various circumstances, some of which is the age factor, another may be based around our timeline for getting engaged, getting married, having families. Ladies, it is imperative that we embrace patience.

We must strive for moral excellence, to be upright, ethical and honest. We cannot be a *hoochie* mama exposing all our body parts from hallelujah to amazing grace. Women young and old should not expose their bodies in garments so tight the seams are screaming, walking around braless and in skin tight micro mini skirts and dresses. This type of dress is inappropriate especially for Christian women. Let's not forget that this is an age of promiscuity of which we must avoid. None of these attributes will gain us favor from God nor attract a <u>godly</u> man.

Again let me remind you that God is not impressed by our outside as much as he is about the inside reflecting him. We have become real "deep" over the years. We teach women how to look holy but we fail to teach them how to live holy. We have commercialized and practiced religion instead of living CHRIST and we turn people off. If a woman does not dress the way we think she should we judge their salvation by their appearance. We can be so pompous and superficial by condemning the less fortunate and ridiculing those who might be doing better than us resulting in battles within the ministry; the "have" against the "have not."

This kind of foolishness and strife is not only a tum-off to men but to God also. It is so important that we take the time to love and teach women to love themselves while allowing time for God to change them and the rest comes easy. When one has the heart of God they become spiritually minded and ready to receive the things of God. With a desire to please God appearance, attitude, character all falls into place.

CHAPTER FOUR

THE SELF-ESTEEM FACTOR

How do you feel about yourself? Do you feel pretty? Do you love yourself? Has past hurts destroyed your inner-person? We need to feel good about ourselves before others can see the good we have to give. It is so important that we receive God's forgiveness before we can forgive and expect others to forgive. As women of faith we must build ourselves up on our inner most faith and strengths.

Self-esteem is simply how we view ourselves. Try this exercise; on a sheet of paper make two columns, one for positives and one for negatives. Now list all of the good qualities you think you have under the positive column and under the negative column list the things you do not like about yourself. For example, some women are displeased with their personal appearance, feet are too big, skin tone is too light or too dark, hips are too wide or, legs too skinny. Now, before you go any further make sure this is an honest assessment because I am going to help you with something but I can only do it if you can be honest. Our view can be clearly intensified when we write things down.

The development of our self-image begins very early in life. Negative things that are deposited in our young spirits can make a negative or positive impact. If you are constantly told that you are stupid, you will soon believe it and more than likely act the part well. If you are told you will never succeed or will never amount to anything because you happen to resemble a relative (your dad of whom you did not choose) and who never succeeded, you won't. If you are teased about your physical make-up, always being compared to others and talked down to you will find yourself always trying to measure up to others expectations.

You may have experienced emotional and physical traumas that cause you to look down on yourself. Traumas such as molestation, incestuous acts, rape, and negative events you witnessed as a child that haunt you and causes constant emotional turmoil and confusion. You cannot be successful if you take these things into a relationship.

Review your list, the negative things you listed were probably brought to your attention by other people, expressed to you during your childhood or during numerous failed relationships. Some of the items on the list can be improved while others like the size of our feet, the shape of our legs, the texture of our hair or the color of our skin is ours for life. So how do we get past these "things" that hinder us and cause us to feel less than? How do we rid ourselves of the things that keep us from being whole? I am so glad you asked. Deliverance through Jesus Christ! If we are not delivered from the effects of negative influences they will keep us from life's successes, hindering us on our job, in our relationships with family, in our relationship with our spouse and in our relationship with God. I refer to these hindrances as "excess baggage" in another book.

First, we must accept the fact that our baggage is a hindrance, an obstacle, and a stronghold that the enemy now uses as stumbling blocks. It has been around for a long time and are strong elements of our mindset.

When we recognize what causes us to feel negatively we need to work on releasing it and casting it out in Jesus' name so we can be free and controlled by the things of God and be made whole.

Sometimes our baggage becomes a crutch and we use the experiences as excuses for our failures. Rather than rising above them we smother ourselves with the experiences and host pity parties to gain sympathy and attention of those around us. This serves no positive purpose and consequently we build barriers that continuously hinder our life's successes.

In the fifth chapter of John we find an interesting event, the healing at the pool of Bethesda. There were a great number of disabled people lying by the pool; they were blind, lame and paralyzed. Once a year an Angel of God would come and trouble the water or stir the pool and those who got in were healed. There was a man lying by the pool that had been there for 38 years. When Jesus asked him, "Do you want to get well?" The man replied that when he tried to get in one would go before him. Jesus told him, "Get up! Pick up your mat and walk."

This is intriguing because the man did not even know who Jesus was. He did not see him as a healer because he was focused on the curative powers of the water. Normally faith in Jesus was essential to cure and while Jesus usually healed because of one's faith, he was not limited by a person's lack of faith.

What am I saying here? Hindrances may have been a part of your life for many years and you may have never realized it and maybe you have. But more importantly is that you do know Jesus and you know that there is no failure in Him. From this point on you can walk free from those ugly negative things that have tormented and distorted your way of thinking. You get up and take up your bed of low self-esteem and be healed. God is a deliverer.

<u>Say this prayer:</u>

Father God in heaven, I release everything, that has caused me to have a low self-image and I rebuke the enemy and the tools he uses to make me feel I have no self-worth. In the name of Jesus, I cast down every stronghold and anything that is not like you. I curse its root and command it to come out! By the Blood of Jesus I am from this moment totally and completely whole and healed in Jesus name Amen.

To continue experiencing this deliverance you must look at things differently than you have in the past. You must see yourself as a beautiful person not just on the outside but on the inside.

You must realize that God created you in His image and therefore everything He made was and is GOOD. Begin to feed your spirit positive things. Saturate yourself with the Word of God and divorce yourself from things and people that feed off the negativity you carried around with you for so many years.

You no longer have to please other people just so you can fit into their world. You fit because God says you do. Do what makes you happy as long as it does not offend or is contrary to God's Word. Remember, these negative feelings may have festered inside of you for years slowly eating at your emotions keeping you from being who you are destined of God to be.

Know this – if it is not of God it is certainly of the enemy. God does not give us the spirit of fear and timidity. He gives us a spirit of power and love and of a sound mind. The psalmist David wrote in Psalm 26:2 *Test me O Lord, and try me, examine my heart and my mind; for your love is ever before me, and I walk continually in your truth.* David keeps his mind and heart continuously focused on the Lord's love and truth, which are pledged to those who keep the demands of his covenant. We must walk continually with Christ in order to receive the covenant benefits.

Psalm 55:22 says: Cast *your cares on the Lord and he will sustain you; He will never let the righteous fall.*

We can give all our concerns, anxieties and worries give them *all* over to Jesus because he cares for us. Think of yourself as having a new body, having a new mind, new thoughts, new concepts, new ideas, all based on the principles of God's teaching. We are no longer the "old" person. We are no longer insecure and we have stepped up and out of the pit of low self-esteem and now see our self as a child of the risen King. If we are walking upright before God then in Him, regardless of what anyone says we are beautiful, inside and out. We are desirable and intelligent and can succeed at whatever we put our mind to doing.

Paul said in Phil. 4:13; "I can do all things through Christ who gives me strength. Romans 8:37 says, "No, in all these things we are more than conquerors through him who loved us."

By the blood of Jesus, we are made whole and complete in Him. Hallelujah!

HOW IS YOUR HYGIENE?

CHAPTER FIVE

THE HYGIENE FACTOR

Well, I guess you are wondering if I am really going there. Yes, I am! Someone has got to go there so it might as well be me. I am known to be a rebel for good causes. There is no valid excuse for ladies to have personal hygiene problems but many do. They have varied reasons. Lack of exposure to good hygiene practices could be a culprit, or they could be lazy and trifling and just uncaring but whatever the reason we must practice good hygiene. This is essential there is just no getting around it.

People use to have all sorts of reasons or excuses for having poor hygiene and at one time many were valid. Some are allergic to various skin cleansers and deodorants but now we have hypoallergenic products. Some were raised with large families in conditions of poverty and may not have been privy to the necessary essentials for their personal hygiene. But what is the excuse today? I realize in other countries, customs are different which affect the hygiene of its inhabitants but we are in America. Our custom is and has been for as long as we have been alive based on the old cliché', "cleanliness is next to godliness."

So you are probably wondering what this has to do with women and the selection process it has everything to do with it. It is offensive to those around us when we have poor hygiene in particularly body odor. If we constantly have body odor it can be assumed that we are not a very clean person and the assumption is an acceptable one.

Women should bathe or shower regularly, wear clean clothes, change our undergarments daily, use deodorant and perfumed fragrances (not too heavy) so we can be pleasing to be near. If not, we will undoubtedly be one of the many offensive smelly females that walk this earth. There is no other way of putting it. This is a sensitive subject but it has to be dealt with if anyone is planning to be joined together in holy matrimony. Good hygiene practices are vital even if we are not in a relationship.

At the age of twelve I began my menses and so had a lot of my friends. Girls talked as girls will and I discovered many did not bathe or shower during this time. Their parents believed in an old wives tales that immersion in water during this time would increase the menses flow or intensify the cramps. So during a time of the month that water and soap is badly needed girls were taking "monkey bathes" or no bathes at all and consequently everyone's nose knew. Many women today are still keeping this practice. STOP...please funk is not friendly! You do not want that kind of reputation. Females need to bathe or shower at least once a day on a normal basis but especially during our cycles to manage odor.

Personal hygiene has been a problem as long as I can remember; in school, at work, and even in church. But I do not think I need to give any more graphic details. No matter how big and burly, or thin and short the man; regardless of the kind of work they do they are definitely attracted to cleanliness. All else is a definite turn-off. If you have good personal hygiene practices, keep it up, if you need to step up in this area just do it. Everyone you know will be so happy that you did.

CHAPTER SIX

A MATCH MADE IN HEAVEN

"Do not be yoked together with unbelievers. For what do righteousness and wickedness have in common? Or what fellowship can light have with darkness? 2 Corinthians 6:14

When we do things God's way we reap the benefits of his promises. God is not going to place us in a relationship of complexity and uncertainty when we walk upright before him. A union made by God will not fail as long as He remains the head of the household and the relationship.

As mentioned in an earlier chapter, women often make the mistake of marrying the wrong person out of desperation. Every man that *tries to get with you* is not sent from God. There are some real "rascals" out there. Cunning, suave characters that do and say all of the things women want to hear. Men who know what makes our flesh quiver and our heart throb, they are able to see through our vulnerability and desires; what the woman in you really wants. The end result; we respond to our human emotions and desires rather than responding to the voice of God. Our idea and expectations of a mate paralleled to whom God has chosen for us may not be the same. The difference is we know what we want and God knows what we need.

Half the marriages in the United States end in divorce. The cause is usually one of two reasons: God did not put them together or God did not remain the head of the relationship. When we exclude God from any area of our life we extend an opened door invitation to the enemy. He moves in breeding discord through so many different ways turning our relationships into his playground and the games played end in us losing. A couple that is brought together by God is not exempt from problems. There will be disagreements, misunderstandings and other quandaries, which are common, because aside from being spiritually minded creatures, we are also human in nature.

This is another reason applying the Word of God is important it helps our relationships survive the pitfalls of life.

Mark 10:6-9 "But at the beginning of creation God made them male and female. For this reason a man will leave his father and mother and be united to his wife, and the two will become one flesh. So they are no longer two, but one. Therefore what God has joined together, let no man separate."

God set the grounds for the sanctity of marriage at the beginning of creation. In this verse Jesus goes back to the time before human sin to show God's original intention. God instituted marriage as a great unifying blessing bonding the male and female in his creation.

This is where many couples fall short they do not realize the importance of becoming "one" flesh. There should be no more yours and mine but ours. Marriage is a serious partnership of oneness. It is much more than an extravagant wedding and reception, more than expensive rings and gifts. Marriage is so much more than hanging from chandeliers and experiencing a passionate rumble between the sheets. Marriage goes beyond bridesmaids, groomsmen, candle and flower girls or ring bearers. Its sanctity goes deeper than the lavish showers and parties and all the celebrations we have. There is life after the ceremony. What we do in preparation for the wedding should be equally or more important to what we do after the celebration is over.

You say you want to get married? Are you ready for a lifetime partner, to stay together in love as long as you both shall live? Marriage is not like an old pair of shoes that you discard when they get old and worn and then buy a new pair. You must be willing and able to adjust to one another's differences. When times get difficult you can't head for the hills and abandon the union. God expects us to develop maturity in marriage just as he expects maturation for believers in His word. Marriage is a lifetime agreement between the couple and God. He alone can provide the stability needed through the couple's commitment and the continual application of His word. This is why it is so important ladies do not fish for their mates.

We need a supernatural intervention from God to produce lifetime results. In relationships we should want to maximize the propensity for peace. To attain this, contribution is needed from both parties. How are your communication skills? We are not telepathic creatures and so it is necessary to be able to talk in a civilized manner discussing likes and dislikes. The relationship cannot survive if it is one-sided. Each has an opinion, each has input, it is a union developed by the contributions of both parties.

Matthew 19:4-6 is a valuable tool that should be incorporated early in the marriage. *"Haven't you read," he replied, "But at the beginning the Creator made them male and female," and said, "For this reason a man will leave his father and mother and be united to his wife, and the two will become one flesh." "So they are no longer two, but one. Therefore, what God has joined together, let man not separate."*

Positively and under no circumstance do we let outside parties cause dissention in our relationship. Women as well as men often have real close ties with parents or friends and have often received advice from them regarding various conditions in life. The Word of God states that husband and wife are NOT to allow outsiders to dabble in their business, which in many cases can be a major cause of breakup. This simply means that we must keep family folk out of our business and the world out of our bedroom. We should work out our differences with each other or with an unbiased source such as a licensed Christian counselor or pastor with a <u>healthy</u> attitude towards marriage.

When God sends your mate and unites you in marriage it can work. No matter what is going on in relationships in the world; no matter the statistics on divorce and separation there can be many years of blissful happiness as you grow together in God. The key thing to remember is let your match be made in heaven.

CAN YOU HANDLE BABY MAMA DRAMA?

CHAPTER SEVEN

MARRYING WITH CHILDREN

We must also consider the problems that can arise when we marry with children. It is critical to the longevity of the relationship to keep in the forefront balance and spiritual maturation. The attraction cannot solely be based on or between the couple but the ability to genuinely love the children is equally important.

Neither should we expect the children to automatically blend or accept the spouse as a figure of authority because respect and trust has to be earned through patience, love and positive interaction. This is a sensitive area because children may see the husband as a threat to their relationship with you and consider him as the man you married and nothing more. Do your research and consider every possible scenario. For starters what are his ideals for discipline? Does he communicate well with the children? Is his interaction only when discipline is needed? Should he have other children does he willfully pay child support and have a healthy relationship with them? Always remember, how a man treats his children from other relationships (regardless of the relationship with the mother) is a good indication of how you and your children will be treated. Try not to eagerly take sides against the mother of his other children. Allow them to work their own differences out because there are three sides to a story: his, hers and the truth. It is not a good idea to force the children to accept you as a couple, allow them time to adjust to your bringing a person into their space or you moving them from an environment of familiarity to his place.

Discussing any behavioral, physical or medical challenges and childhood fears the children may have is important. Consider what changes you are going to have to make as a family and include the children so they can freely discuss any concerns they may have. Under no circumstances should we allow a man to abuse our children, psychologically, physically, sexually, verbally or emotionally. This is never acceptable. Should you choose to remain in a dysfunctional unsafe relationship that's on you but do not subject your children to it. It is our responsibility to protect the well fare of our children at all cost.

In addition, be aware that "baby mama drama" can implode once the "X" realizes her baby daddy is going to marry someone else. Her bruised ego can transform her into the "X" from hell. As long as she and her children's father are connected by the children she will be an outside factor inside your family. You and your significant other (husband to be) should thoroughly discuss these issues and project solutions or coping mechanisms before you say, "I do." Since the "X" can create confusion there should be an adhesive agreement between the two of you to prevent her from causing dissention or confusion, in your home.

I've been there and done that so I am fairly knowledgeable of what works and what does not work. When people know that they are going to be required to respect you both and that your relationship cannot be breeched you dislodge the propensity for baby mama or baby daddy drama. In other words the only sides that should be taken are you and your rib. Your business problems, financial or personal problems should not be discussed with an "X." The only conversation should be regarding the rearing of the children they have together. Visitations should not exclude you. Some men want their cake and eat it too. You will be the wife and should never be excluded from interactions he may have with his children's mother.

Marrying with children and avoiding baby mama drama needs to be thoroughly discussed and he should make sure that his children's mother knows his stance and loyalty is with you.

CHAPTER EIGHT

TEN PRINCIPLES FOR WOMEN

As we walk in our destiny we must have a plan. It is not wise just to walk aimlessly around while you wait to be found. We need to know where we have been and likewise know where we are going. But more importantly know how you are going to get there. Wishful thinking will not help us reach our goals, neither can we pray and leave everything up to God. We need goals. Once we pray we then must activate our faith even before we petition God in prayer. Believe it to be already done and stand on God's Word and his promises. A youth pastor once preached a message titled, "Every Promise Has a Now." When God makes a promise to us it is as good as done. All we need to do is activate our faith and stand firm on what His Word promises. Remember, God blesses the things that we do, not the things we conjure up with our emotions or thoughts.

James 2:26 As the body without the spirit is dead, so faith without deeds (works) is dead.

Work cannot replace prayer and prayer alone will not replace works. It is not enough to pray for a mate but we must work at being who Good needs us to be. Ready and in position to accept being a mate. By working I am not implying that we go fishing. There are other ways we can work at being in position. Searching on our own is like looking for a needle in a haystack because who we find will not be who God has destined for us. Because we see with the natural eye we cannot see into the debts of a man's heart. As I have said before, we may meet men that say and do all the right things according to our desires and expectations: fashionable dresser, handsome, nice body, smooth conversation with flattering words all of which are great expectations but can also prove to be superficial. We see things that we want to see, things that to the natural eye make one desirable to another. But to spiritually know whom the man is that God wants for us is what God knows best.

The following are ten principles that will help guide you so you do not lose focus.

Ten Principles for Women

1. Pray fervently for a husband but don't beg.

2. Avoid promiscuous behavior.

3. Surround yourself with wise, competent people.

4. Follow your heart.

5. Allow God to give you the same qualities you are looking for in a man.

6. Be skilled domestically, secure a good education and develop some type of skill.

7. Be a good steward over your finances.

8. Be able to forgive and say, "I am sorry."

9. Go into the relationship with the mindset of being no longer two, but one.

10. Do not let your expectations overpower the reality of your relationship.

1. Pray fervently for a husband but don't beg

James 5:16 Therefore confess your sins to each other and pray for each other so that you may be healed. The prayer of a righteous man is powerful and effective.

There is no need to pray out of a spirit of desperation but let your prayers be earnest from the depths of your heart. Come to God and just ask him for what you want. Be certain when you pray that your heart and motive is pure. If you are living righteous and upright before God you can come before Him in earnest. Some approach with a begging spirit because they know that they are coming to God as a mischievous child not really expecting results because of disobedience but hoping that mercy will be had and their request may be granted.

When my children were small as a parent I knew there were things that were not good for them. As an example, as all children they loved candy. They never seemed to get enough the more they ate the more they wanted. Small children cannot see beyond their craving for the sweet taste of candy. They do not realize that although candy taste good; too much is not good for them. Over indulgence can cause health problems and decayed teeth. At times my children would beg and scheme for candy but I would not always give in to their whining because as a parent I knew what was best for them.

It is the same with God, He is our Father and because we do not know what our future holds we can be certain that God knows what is best for us, and when is the best time for him to give us what we ask for, if at all.

Psalm 27:13-14 I am still confident of this: I will see the goodness of the Lord in the land of the living. Wait for the Lord; be strong and take heart and wait for the Lord.

When events do not transpire in the timing we would like for them to there is no need to beg. Begging will not speed God up nor make him change his mind. The important thing to do is live holy and righteous before him. Only those who know and do the Lord's will should expect to receive favorable responses to prayers. So rather than coming before the Lord begging come before him in confidence, believing you will receive your request in this life.

2. Avoid Promiscuous Behavior

Galatians 5:19-21 The acts of sinful nature are obvious: sexual immorality, impurity and debauchery; idolatry and witchcraft; hatred, discord, jealousy, fits of rage, selfish ambition, dissensions, factions and envy; drunkenness, orgies, and the like. I warn you, as I did before, that those who live like this will not inherit the kingdom of God.

Celibacy for single women is essential to living holy and righteous. Promiscuity is a problem not only in the world but also in the church. We still have women young and old living under the bondage of sexual sin. Women are involved in sexual sin for various reasons. Some feel that if they sleep with a man before matrimony it will seduce him into marriage. Others believe if they move in together and become comfortable marriage will be inevitable. But there is an old adage, "Why buy the cow when you can get the milk free?" Why we allow our flesh to rule us and influence us to give in to premarital sex is perplexing. Although we know the consequences we are only concerned with pleasure and satisfying our uncontrollable urges. Others sleep around because they are foolish enough to only be concerned with not getting caught by man, ignoring the fact that God sees everything we do and he is the most impressionable. Face it! We have a problem!

Promiscuous living has negative results. For one it taints our anointing and separates us from God.

The Holy Spirit who dwells within the believer produces Christian character as well as produces Christian virtues in the believers' life.

Aside from not having self-respect, others lose respect for us also including our sexual partner(s). There is always the chance of contracting sexually transmitted diseases, many of which have no cure and the disease and treatment can have devastating effects. The chance of children being born into a godless union creating a single-parent environment for the child is also of concern. The most damaging to ones character as a believer is that your sin affects the testimony of the church.

Galatians 5:22-26 We must live by the fruit of the Spirit, which is love, joy, peace, patience, kindness, goodness, faithfulness, gentleness and self-control. Against such things there is no law. Those who belong to Christ Jesus have crucified the sinful nature with its passions and desires. Since we live by the Spirit let us keep in step with the Spirit. Let us not become conceited, provoking and envying each other.

3. Surround yourself in the company of wise, competent and godly people.

Psalm 1:1 Blessed is the man that walketh not in the counsel of the ungodly, nor standeth in the way of sinners nor sitteth in the seat of the scornful. But his delight is in the law of the Lord; and in his law doth he meditate day and night.

This is good advice because if we desire a godly man we too must have a godly character. It is important that as we are preparing ourselves we do not find ourselves in the wrong company, whether at church, work or school. We know people by their character and this is what will speak well or negatively of us. A godly woman walks not in the council of the ungodly. This character trait shows wisdom and she will wisely turn away from evil. Ungodly people do not fear God.

Sinners they are openly rebellious against God and their heart is so hardened that they mock religion and sin. God blesses the godly and in doing so it brings about happiness.

<u>Romans 14:16</u> the bible says:
Let *not to let your good be evil spoken of.*

It is important that we choose our friends wisely including those we "hang out" with. Character, integrity and accountability are important, especially if we are striving to live by example. Once we become implicated in an evil deed or scandal our reputation is at stake and our testimony is challenged. It is judicious to be mindful of this as we choose our friends and acquaintances.

4. Follow Your Heart

The Psalmist David wrote in Psalm 119:11, *"Thy word have I hid in my heart, that I might not sin against thee."*

<u>In the Matthew Henry Commentary we find this:</u>

David applied the word of God to himself: *He hid it in his heart,* laid it up there, that it might be ready to him whenever he had occasion to use it. He laid it up as that which he valued highly, and had a warm regard for, and which he was afraid of losing and being robbed of. God's word is a treasure worth lying up, and there is no safer place to lay it as in our hearts. If we have it only in our houses and hands, enemies may take it from us; if only in our heads, our memories may fail us: but if our hearts be delivered into the mold of it, and the impressions of it remain on our souls, it is safe. *That I might not sin against thee.* Good men are afraid of sin, and are in care to prevent it; and the most effectual way to prevent is to hide God's word in our hearts, that we may answer every temptation with affirmation in Him.

If your heart has stored up in it the Word of God, your thoughts and decisions will be made from a godly point of view. Your heart will follow God's heart.

God's Word is our avenue for retrieval of his will for our lives. His word provides the tools we need for daily living.

When God's Word is embedded in us we are able to access spiritual discernment and our choices are made according to his principles. Physical attributions or material possessions do not easily fool us or cause us to lose focus from the truth of what God has for us.

5. Allow God to give you the same qualities you are looking for in a man.

God is a God of righteousness and all he does is just and right. This means that God is fair. It would not be fair for him to give us a mate with the qualities and character we do not have.

As earlier mentioned women usually have great expectations when it comes to marriage, especially Christian women and there is nothing wrong with that. As we mature we began to dream about marriage, owning a home with a yard and having children. The focus is usually on being with a handsome man, educated with a secure job and financial status. We desire someone that is kind, thoughtful, honest, sincere, affectionate, humorous, sensual and tender. We desire a man who will be good with children and family oriented. One way to insure we are matched up with a man with fine qualities is to be sure that we are all that we are looking for. If God is allowed to work on our heart and spirit He can mold and shape us. Take inventory and honestly see whether you have these same qualities especially women who are independent and have been taking care of yourself for a long period of time. While waiting we can become complacent or set in our ways. There is a strong chance for us to become selfish and self-absorbed. A spirit of bitterness and mistrust can harbor within us because of past dysfunctional relationships.

There is a possibility, if we are not mindful of the things of God we will become the very opposite of what we desire. Concentrate on the things of God so He can mold us into the kind of woman we need to be for the kind of man we desire.

6. **Be domestic, get a good education and develop some type of skill.**

Being domestic does not mean being a slave to house work. It simply means that you have the ability to take care of the needs of your house to make it a home. You can prepare balanced meals that are tasty to the palette; you can handle a simple chore like doing laundry and know what clothes wash well together. Being neat and clean is also important. These responsibilities can be shared but we need to know how to maintain a household.

While we are waiting on our mate we can occupy our time by furthering our education to obtain a degree in the field of our choice. We may choose not to work but it is good to be prepared if the need becomes necessary. If we do not choose to further our education by attending college by all means complete high school and learn a respectable trade.

Remember the parable of the five wise virgins and the five foolish virgins (Matthew 25:1-13). Five were prepared to meet the bridegroom and five were not. The five foolish had not purchased enough oil to take them through the procession and wanted the five wise maids to share their oil with them. While the five foolish were out trying to purchase oil they missed the procession as well as the wedding banquet.

I realize that the main point of the parable is that we stay ready for the coming of Christ but it also teaches a valuable lesson for us to be prepared in every area of life. God just may be trying to get you into the position of preparedness.

7. Be a good steward over your finances

There are so many women and men that are financially challenged due to poor stewardship. A steward is one that is in charge of households or estates, or one who manages household accounts. The key here is not so much that you have been given the authority but that you are responsible. Men and women get caught in the clutches of debt. There is nothing wrong with debt as long as we are able to fulfill our daily financial obligations without strain or having to go deeper into debt to get relief. God does not want us bound by debt. Debt is a tool of the enemy it is not of God. Remember *3 John 2 Beloved, I wish above all things that thou mayest prosper and be in health, even as thy soul prospereth.*

Oftentimes Christians have mistaken this as a promise of continuous wealth and health. But this was a common phrase used in the everyday language and was so popular it was often referred to by initials. The word prospers meant to "have a good journey." John was writing to Gaius who had been sharing his home with traveling prophets.

We should always remember that God does want the best for us, and often presents material prosperity and physical health as a part of that good He has for us. Yet God may according to His divine plan use a lack of material prosperity and physical health to promote greater prosperity and health in days to come. Think about it! What if your physical health was in the same state as your spiritual health, many would be in trouble. John's good will towards Gaius comes because he knows that that Gaius is walking in truth.

So if you want to be prosperous we have to begin with being honest. Stop living a financial lie! Take authority over your finances and get out of debt so that you can live in comfort and in peace.

8. Be able to forgive and say, "I'm sorry."

One of the most difficult things for two opposing people to do is for one to admit being wrong or to say, "I am sorry." Being willing to do this does not make one weak but moreover suggests that one is strong because they have the ability to be humble in a situation gone wrong. Apologizing does not admit to any wrong action but on the contrary lets the other person know you love them and regret doing or saying anything that may have offended them.

On the downside you do not want to be the one who is always asking forgiveness for doing wrong or saying something in the heat of a disagreement that you regret. Continued physical or emotional abuse does not show love but more so that one may have a serious emotional problem. Words can hurt.

Just as we are reminded in scripture to have a spirit of repentance we likewise will find it necessary at times to repent one to another in relationship.

Being able to say, "I'm sorry" can often diffuse a heated moment by breaking down defense barriers opening the door to shared communication.

9. Go into the relationship with the mindset of being no longer two, but one.

Genesis 2:23-24 The man said, "This is bone of my bones and flesh of my flesh; she shall be called woman, for she was taken out of man." For this reason a man will /eave his father, and mother and unite to his wife, and they will become one flesh.

Leaving the home of parents a man leaves, with his wife and establishes a new family unit. Together they form an inseparable union of which "one flesh" is both a sign and an expression.

There is no more need for separate bank accounts, hidden agendas or private credit cards. It is a good sign that if you do not feel you can trust your mate to be one flesh in every area of your life, including finances you probably need to reconsider matrimony.

It is so much easier when you can work together and when you can trust your mate to do right by you. Trust is very important and a relationship based on such is essential. If either of you enters into the relationship with thoughts of being divided, in any area, you cannot function in God's will. Furthermore, you open the door for Satan to come in causing confusion and destruction.

Lastly, God's plan is for a union of undivided flesh because His Spirit cannot flow amongst division and strife.

10. Do not let your expectations overpower the reality of your relationship

Blessed is the man who finds wisdom, the man who gains understanding. Proverbs 3:13

Divine wisdom comes from God and a wise woman is more precious than jewels. Be wise and reasonable in your expectations of your relationship. If you can successfully master the last nine principles the sky is the limit. But if you fall short in any area you may be expecting more than is reasonable. Be spiritual in this area so that you are not blinded by your fleshly desires. Who God has for you may not shine like gold or silver. Your mate may be the opposite of whom you thought or desired him to be. Remember God's selection process is not based on our wants but on our need.

In closing out this chapter I will share a personal story with you to help you better understand how God works, oftentimes beyond our natural understanding. Prior to my last marriage I was hurt and endured a lot of emotional trauma. Things you just do not think can happen to you – sometimes happen. After an inclement divorce I was left devastated.

The reality of having to start my life over after nineteen years was overwhelming. But, there was one thing I knew for sure, I would never marry again. I had not concerned myself with God's divine plan just what I wanted and did not want.

My husband (now deceased) and I had been the best of friends for at least twelve years, crossing each other's paths in ministry from time to time. He was definitely not my choice for a mate. To make a long story short God placed us together and he was the best thing aside from being saved and filled with the Holy Ghost that has come into my life. We spiritually complemented one another and we worked very close together in ministry all for the cause of Christ. Were we one flesh? Yes, we certainly were. Did we operate as one in the spirit? Yes we did. We had differences of opinions and did not always see eye to eye on matters, but the key to our thriving relationship was God joined us together. Practicing bible principles daily sustained us and took us through many difficult times. We learned how to accept becoming mates by allowing God to begin preparing us before we were joined together in marriage.

Apply these principals to your life as you allow God to prepare you for that special someone.

CHAPTER NINE

THE CONCLUSION OF THE WHOLE MATTER

Ladies, stop fishing! No good thing will come from you trying to help God do what he does best.

Ecclesiastes 3:1-8 There is a time for everything, and a season for every activity under heaven: A time to be born and a time to die, a time to plant and a time to uproot, a time to kill and a time to heal, and time to tear down and a time to build, a time to weep and a time to laugh, a time to mourn and a time to dance, a time to scatter stones and a time to gather them, a time to embrace and a time to refrain, a time to search and a time to give up, a time to keep and a time to throw away, a time to tear, and a time to mend, a time to be silent and a time to speak, a time to love and a time to hate, a time for war and a time for peace.

These scriptures reveal to us that we have little or no control over times and changes and that God's eternity and sovereignty predetermine all of life's activities. We must realize that there is a time for all things but a divinely appointed time for them. As Christian women we can find meaning in life when we readily accept it from the hand of God.

Oftentimes and especially in this new era women want to do things their way. This is the age of high technological advancement, the age of the corporate woman and the age of equality, women are actually placing themselves on a scale of measurement to be equal to men. Regardless of whom it affects we tend to be continuously driven to do things our way. This is why we get into so much trouble and experience so many disappointments; we are negligent in allowing everything to have its season or its divine timing.

Let's dig a little deeper into the matter. When we do things according to God's divine plan the margin for error is non-existent. The results are not doom and disaster as when we do things our way. The ideal plan in life for women would be to complete your education on through high school and then go on to college mastering a profession if the latter is your desire. We should establish ourselves in life's responsibilities, which over a period of time constitutes self-discipline and teaches us to be reliable. When things are done in divine order we set ourselves up to receive the blessings of God. Many say it is a new era and so we do things differently. We feel the ways of old have outdated themselves and a new way is needed to accomplish our goals of today.

Change is good and in many cases is necessary to keep up with our societal pace. But we preference change because for us the ways of old require too much patience and thought, too much time and energy. We want things now or sooner than that. Being rational is an afterthought that comes much too late to act upon. This new way of thinking can prove destructive.

Instead of following a pattern that is based on bible principles which, will more likely work on our behalf we follow patterns that actually work against us. Sex is instituted for marriage but on the contrary we are driven daily by our fleshly nature and become sexually active oftentimes very early in life. We are influenced by pornography and sexually explicit messages sent out in the media, on television, at the movies and in things we choose to read. There are an alarming number of teens and adult women who are contracting sexually transmitted diseases and the number of babies being born out of wedlock is still at an all-time high. For the teens it means that they continue their education in alternative schools (a joke education), more than likely not completing high school at all, living with their parent(s), relative or boyfriend, raising a child as a single parent with no skills or education having to be supported by their local welfare system. These actions are neither unplanned nor pre-planned. Women and young girls are choosing to have children outside of marriage.

From a statistical report prepared by The National Campaign to Prevent Teen Pregnancy these facts are indicative of an ongoing problem. The United States has the highest rates of teen pregnancy and births. Four in 10 young women become pregnant at least once before the age of 20. Eight in ten of these pregnancies are intended and 79 percent are to unmarried teens. Teen mothers are less likely to complete high school and more likely to end up on welfare. Their babies have lower birth rates, do poorly in school and are at greater risk of abuse and neglect.

Paul wrote in a letter to the Corinthian church in regards to questions he was being asked about marriage. The Corinthian church had many problems dealing with morality and marriage, because of the corrupt pagan society in which they lived.

1 Corinthians 7:1-2 Now concerning the things whereof ye wrote unto me: It is good for a man not to touch a woman. Nevertheless, to avoid fornication, let every man have his own wife, and let every woman have her own husband.

Paul said it was a good thing for a Christian to be celibate, meaning single and completely abstinent from sex. Paul suggested marriage as a preventative to fornication but the purpose of his teaching was not teaching that the only purpose for marriage was to prevent fornication. Paul was trying to demonstrate that sexual relationship was God's good gift to marriage.

What we should do regarding our teens and young adult women is educate them before they make us grandparents. We do not need to educate them on the use of contraceptives but what the Word says in regards to sexual activity. I strongly feel that if parents in the church are negligent the church needs to get its head out the sand and educate our youth, protecting them against the temptation that the enemy has boldly placed before them.

Remember, doing things our way discarding the things of God causes us to step outside of His will and began traveling a road of destruction. Our fleshly ways just cause more and more problems. Look at the farmer. Everything that is harvested has a season for planting.

When planted in season and given favorable weather conditions the farmer is sure to yield a bountiful crop. But if planting is done out of season he will not yield bountifully. Doing things out of its season seems fashionable to the new age woman. We have our children and seek child support as a means of income. Then we decide to put the child in daycare or leave them in the care of a relative or friend to be raised while we continue our education and pursue careers. How backwards is this?

While waiting on God we become impatient and we begin to believe, as the enemy would have it, that there will be no mate or matrimony, so we skip to the next phase. We begin executing our own plans, with our own purpose and then time and time again worry God through our prayer petitions to get us out of the mess we made.

Psalm 84:11 For the Lord God is a sun and shield; the Lord bestows favor and honor; no good things does he withhold from those whose walk is blameless.

God is the source of our life and if we walk upright before him we will receive favor from him and he will honor us. Stop fishing!

I need to share one more very **important** note. If you are saved and interested in an unsaved man that is not of God. You can best believe that your job is not to play God. Only He can save us through confessed belief on His Son Jesus Christ. Again! That is not your job! Saved women associate with unsaved men because they are desperate. God does not lead you in that direction while you are waiting to be found. This premise totally contradicts His Word.

If you and your *boo* breakup before you can get to the altar and then he returns because his other choice did not work out, don't be foolish, put the brakes on. This may have been God's way of protecting you from pain and disappointment. Remember why he is an "X."

Numbers 23:19 God is not a man that he should lie, nor a son of man that he should change his mind. Does he speak and then not act? Does he promise and not fulfill?

These noble words describe the steadfastness of the Lord and the completeness of his Word. He does not constantly shift, falsifying, deceitfully changing—a prime example of the distinction between God and man. His word is true and it does not change. There is a godly man just for you, but you must have patience while waiting on God to manifest this in your life.

Abide in God's will so you will be in position to accept being a mate. Do your part and remember what we discussed in the previous chapters, review if you need to. Walk confidently knowing that you are somebody in Christ. Promiscuity and hypocrisy are not an option but moreover are a means to self-destruction so strive to live holy and righteous.

Be encouraged as you live saved and have a noble character, be virtuous and wise. Walk by Faith and not by what you see. Allow your footsteps to be ordered by God and not by the circumstances set before or behind you. God has your mate and he is preparing you both like diamonds in the rough, being chiseled and polished to perfection so your relationship will honor and glorify him.

Fishing can result in catching anything and everything; but only God can bait our spiritual hooks and give us the catch of a lifetime. Ladies remember…no more fishing!

Ladies No More Fishing

RESOURCES

Bureau of Justice Prison Statistics.gov

Guzik, David Commentary. Blue Letter Bible.Org,

Henry, Matthew Commentary. Blue Letter Bible.Org.

National Campaign to Prevent Teen Pregnancy.com

Smith, Chuck. Blue Letter Bible.Org,

Wikepedia.org. Encyclopedia. 2010

Wikipedia.org. Thesaurus. 2010

Ladies No More Fishing

ABOUT THE AUTHOR

One of her favorite past times is writing and providing office and graphic services through The Fantasy Graphics a small home-based business. Another enjoyment is teaching and ministering to the needs of women.

Her spiritual coverings that were life changing were under Grace Unlimited Ministries with Pastors Melvin and April Jackson where she was licensed as a minister and served with her late husband as executive pastor and Church of the Word – South Bay where she was ordained as an elder and served as executive pastor on the executive board and executive team of this ministry and her senior and co-Pastors were Henry & Alicia Pigee'. Currently her membership is with Worship Center Community Church – Long Beach, California, a vastly growing ministry with Pastor Sheridan E. & First Lady Larleslie McDaniel.

Shiela is one of four children and the only girl, the mother of three children; Denzil, Chisa and Damien and a proud grandmother of, Ashley and Trinity. Along with her late husband it was discovered in 2006 he had a twenty-three year old daughter named Tony and three beautiful grandchildren, "Q," and twin boys Imari and Amir born in March 2007 (six months before his death).

Her favorite past time is writing including but not limited to: plays, poems, gospel music, books, and magazine articles. She is currently a writer for the Antelope Valley Sentinel.

Shiela received her AA degree at East Los Angeles College in the P.A.C.E. program where she instituted a student newsletter, annual can drive and graduation banquet. Her BA was received at Cal State University, Dominguez Hills and a Masters in Ministry at the California School of Ministry, Los Angeles Campus.

A long term goal is to pursue her Doctorate in Ministry. After spending over 20 years in the music ministry God called her to preach and teach the Gospel. It has not been an easy task for her to continue this path without her husband and best friend.

They worked closely together in ministry, well over eleven years and both had a "spirit of excellence." It is one of many adjustments we sometimes have to make in life but she is determined to continue doing kingdom work.

She is a gift to the Body and community offering much through teaching and preaching from personal experiences, practical principles and through biblical concepts.

Other Teachings….

• How to be Free From Excess Baggage

Her first book, for all that take unresolved, emotional issues from one relationship to another. Life's negative experiences resulting from traumas encountered in childhood and as adults are destructive and result in low and no self-esteem ultimately causing chaotic relationships. We learn why and how we take painful experiences into new relationships better known as "excess baggage," and how to get delivered, be free and know it. Useful materials and handouts are provided with this teaching. This is a powerful deliverance ministry.

• Ladies, No More Fishing

This is a dynamic teaching based on her book targeting women who are seeking God for a mate. She uses biblical and practical principles encouraging women to wait on God to send their mate. When we fish for men we set ourselves up for destructive, unfulfilled, one-sided relationships. Useful materials and handouts are provided with this teaching.

• Do Christians Have to Fall

There are many great men and women who have been tricked and fooled by the enemy some secretly and in the open are caught up in ungodly sinful practices that not only discredit them, but also the Body of Christ. This teaching helps us to understand how and why we fall and also biblically supports that we do not have to. Moreover it teaches how we can keep from falling.

Living Saved and Single…

Celibacy is not an option. For men and women, seriously dating, or engaged.

• I'm Grieving and I Can't Get up

Teaching based on her book, "Surviving the Loss of a Loved One." In a group setting we learn how to understand the grieving process, what to expect during grieving and how to survive it. As she shares the loss of her husband she is transparent with her emotions throughout the grieving process. This can be very beneficial to your congregation to help those who are caught in the grieving cycle, to go through in a healthy manner and come out healthy and victorious. Also teaches us how to recognize danger symptoms, knowing what to do when they experience "melt downs" and where to look for additional help if needed. Useful materials and handouts are provided with this teaching.

• Recipe for a Good Marriage

With divorce on the rise this is great biblical teaching on saving the institution of marriage. What causes marriages to fail? Why are spouses unfaithful? Why do we fall out of love so easy and more? Have men and women's rolls switched or changed? Can spouses be faithful? What does the Bible say about Divorce?

• Ministering to Your Pastor

Scriptural and practical teaching why it is important for parishioners to support their ministry and pastor. What happens when we don't support. What does God expect of us? Tithing is not an option…

- **Church Administration & Staff Training**

Teaching includes instructions on how to perform in an effective and efficient manner using up-to-date technology, forms control, software and twenty-first century office procedures. Organizing your work and managing your staff so the ministry operates with a "spirit of excellence."

Elder Shiela Harris is available for teaching, and speaking. Call Touch the World TV & Artist Management at

213-485-7210 or 562-436-9409 or

touchtheworldnow.com

For information and availability

Order Books at Createrspace.com

Also see websites at:

http://churchadministrationtraining.webs.com

www.touchingtheworldnow.com

Ladies No More Fishing
Invincible Woman

By Shiela Harris

They say I am invincible

Because I do not break under pressure

They say I am unbeatable

Because I never give up

They say I am unconquerable

Because I am an army of one

They say I am unshakeable

Because I am not easily surprised

They say I am indomitable

Because of my strength

The say I am impregnable

Because I am divinely protected

They say I am unassailable

Because I am sure of my self-worth

They say I am insuperable

Because I do not run from challenges

They say I am delectable

Because I am insatiable to man

I am incredible

Because I am an invincible woman

www.ingramcontent.com/pod-product-compliance
Lightning Source LLC
Chambersburg PA
CBHW070105100426
42743CB00012B/2654